A NEW ORLEANS VOODOO HERITAGE EDITION

WATERS OF RETURN

The Aeonic Flow of Voudoo

I0078924

DR. LOUIE MARTINIÉ

BLACK MOON PUBLISHING

CINCINNATI, OHIO

U S A

Black Moon Manifesto

It is the Will and mission of Bate Cabal/Black Moon to effectively manifest unique and insightful occult Works for the esoteric community in a manner that is unfettered by commercial considerations.

BlackMoonPublishing.com

Design and layout by
Jo Bounds of Black Moon Publishing, LLC

ISBN: 978-1-890399-65-8

United States • United Kingdom • Europe • Australia • India

FOREWORD

"You want to know if the loa are 'real?'
Well, they are a lot more 'real' than the
United States of America and the U.S.
can kill you."
                                        — Akoko, conversation, 1985

We are composed of flesh and death;
Turn and return,
Begetter of transformations.
                                        — From "IFA, A Yoruba Oracle"

Voudoo sings with a voice long stilled and denegrated by a pernicious racism. It sings to the mind through the formal elegance and deep insight of its theology. It sings to the heart through the beauty and grace of its diverse pantheon of loa (deities). A closed mind and a hardened heart can not hear, much less appreciate, the richness of this religious voice. As surely as the heavens revolve to signal the primacy of new Aeons, as surely as the Great Wheel turns, the time of Voudoo has come again to light the fires of the soul and set them spinning in a dance of immanent creation. We have only to extend the open hand of acceptance to be rewarded with a spiritual sense of estatic participation. The ancient Mysteries uncoil and call to all those who would listen.

This chapbook is intended to serve as an introduction to a branch of the Voudoun which I choose to call Aeonic Voudoo. The body of theory and practices grew from a matrix of ritual work, conversation, and readings. Aeonic Voudoo, while not transmitting a pure current in the traditional sense, draws heavily from traditional sources. Tradition originally meant "a surrender; a betrayal." I take this surrender or betrayal to refer to an

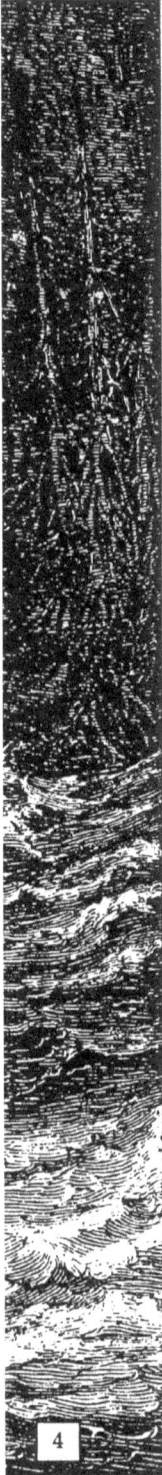

inflexible adherence to that which has gone before. This rigidity is a form of idolatry. Tradition is a heady brew upon which experience feeds. Experience, in its turn, modifies and builds new traditions. We are the ancestors of our children's children. It is our words and works, mixed with the words and works of those who have gone before us, which will be remembered.

The Aeon in which we are presently incarnate has been called by various names. "Aquarian" seems to be the designation which is most widely used in New World cultures. The Aquarian mode emphasizes profound searching, a reliance upon experiential knowledge, and a uniting of diverse occult systems. Aeonic Voudoo seeks to incorporate these dispositions in its structure.

Aeonic Voudoo, in its daily rites of becoming, shows itself in acts/sacraments[1] grounded in five philosophical stances. These are Anarchism; the state of being without a "frozen" hierarchy. Postdrogeny; the abrogation of all existent gender roles so that new perceptions may manifest. Feminism; as it is in the forefront in its stand against restriction and for human liberation. Equalitarianism; the belief that all people have equal political and social rights, and Nonviolence; a refusal to subject the self or others to physical coersion. A sense of community and an active attention to commonality of interest provides a worthy bedrock for all acts.

The Marassa (twins), Morts (the dead), and the Mysteries (loa) constitute the trinity of Aeonic Voudoo. They may be visualized as a trident planted points down in the earth. Through this staff the healing powers of this planet flow to meet the icey fire of the stars.

The Marassa, the Morts, and the Mysteries are as tracings upon the sandy shore of existence. The waves of time come quickly to erase their form. Their form may be lost but their essence is carried, deeply encoded, into the heart of the all surrounding ocean. Lift then this living heart from the breast of the ocean and drink deeply of its eternal essence.

4

---

[1]A sacrament is used to mean an outward sign of an internal state.

THE MARASSA

he Marassa are the Divine Twins; first issue of the Void. Their play is that of duality. They are Lovers locked in an eternal embrace upon the brink of nothingness. Theirs is the existential courage to divide and Be. The creation and reconciliation of distinction is their primary attribute. The winds of the earth and of space, in that these winds are an unseen presence before which all moves, constitute their primary aspect. The praise names of the Marassa are whispered at the very roots of creation.

The duality which is the Marassa[1] finds its most obvious expression in the symmetry which is one of the shared characteristics of all planetary life forms. The parts which comprise this symmetry are nonantagonistic and dependent upon each other for their very existence.

The vèvè,[2] used to call the Marassa is as follows:

Marassa   Crossroads   Combination

---

[1] It is interesting to note that in Gematria the number of the word "Marassa" is the same as a Hebrew word for "two." Marassa: M(40) + R(200) + S(60) + S(60) = 360 = Shin/Nun/Yodh (letters of a Hebrew word for "two"). Shin(300) + Nun(50) + Yodh(10) = 360. (Gematria from SEPHER SEPHIROTH; compiled by Aleister Crowley; et al.)

[2] Vèvè is a ritual drawing of cornmeal, colored chalk, etc. The signature of a loa.

The symmetry of the vèvè is demonstrated when the figure is bisected by a vertical and horizontal line. This is the symmetry of the crossroads. The crossroads is the particular province of Legba, opener of the door between the worlds and messenger of the loa. A powerful ritual current can be created by drawing the Marassa vèvè and then bisecting the vèvè on the horizontal and vertical to call Legba. In this manner, the Marassa (duality) give birth to Legba (the word). The Marassa shine forth from the center of the crossroads.

Drumming in ritual is of great importance. In a sense, the rhythmic combinations are part of the loa's "naming." Rhythm can be understood as the alternation of sound and silence. Different combinations of sound and silence aide in the calling forth of the various Loa. The bibliography lists recordings on which examples of ritual drumming can be heard.

The drum beats which I have found to be appropriate to the Marassa have two pronounced qualities. First of all, they emphasize the distinction between sound and silence. Silence is not simply an empty space between beats. It is an important feature of the rhythmic formation. The silences in the rhythm are deserving of complete attention. This is quite difficult. The usual musical strategy is to attend to the sound and, at best, wait through the silences. By extension, the rhythms of the Marassa are an exercise in attention to action and the spaces that exist between acts. One can use these rhythms to become adept in creating relationships to existent/nonexistent states. Secondly, the Marassa are childlike in their play. The rhythms have a simple, childlike quality.

The Legba that comes to me has the attributes of a wise elder. The gait of the loa is characterized by steady determination and a pronounced limp originating in the right leg. Legba's rhythms are steady and carry the weight of timeless experience. This loa is the master of language and as such has a wit and a sense of humor that is truly astounding. This wit and humor is expressed in "fills" interspersed within the main body of the rhythm.

Skill and technique are important in ritual drumming. Traditional drummers spend a lifetime learning and perfecting a multitude of beats. While recognizing the importance of technique, it is possible to drum directly from the spirit. The loa, while being exact in their dealings, greatly reward even small accomplishment.

There are many stories relating the origin of the twins. Perhaps a Yoruba legend is most worth telling. I will relate it in a much shortened form.

In ancient times there was a man who was a farmer. At his touch the fields sprang to life and the crops were abundant. The monkeys of the region plagued the farmer. They came again and again taking much of the produce. In anger, the farmer killed the monkeys who came onto the fields. Still the monkeys persisted.

The farmer's anger grew and he began to hunt the monkeys in the bush and the forest. Many monkeys were killed yet the crops continued to be depleted.

The monkeys, in their turn, grew angry and two of them entered the womb of the woman who was wife to the farmer. The two monkeys came as abukus, or children who die soon after birth. Up to this time, only the monkeys birthed twins. This was the first instance of twinned birth among the Yoruba. The twins, being abukus, soon died. They entered the woman time and time again, and each time they died soon after birth.

The woman and the man were desperate and consulted a diviner. They were told that the twins came from the monkeys. The killing of the monkeys had to cease and the monkeys were to be allowed to feed on the crops. They accepted this advice and the following set of twins lived. The twins had great powers and caused the farm to prosper. Because of their origin the twins are often called edun, meaning monkey.

— From "Tales of the Yoruba"

An element of a kernel myth, which predates the tales' agricultural time frame, may be discerned here. The twins originated from the monkeys. We now suspect that the first hominoids branched from simian stock. In this genetic branching, our initial hominoid ancestors may have perished time and time again before their survival was assured by an appropriate mutation. Haitian Voudoun **(Divine Horsemen)** names the Marassa as our first ancestors. It is interesting to note that the Yoruba have the highest rate of twinning on the planet.

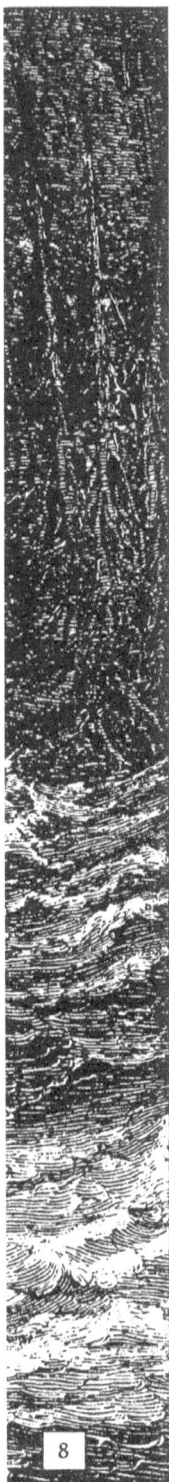

THE MORT

The Mort are the Dead; both named and forgotten. Among their ranks are numbered deceased ancestors. The dead wait in the abysmal waters which ebb and flow beneath the earth. In these waters they wait and watch and, if bidden, reach out with sure fingers to guide and regulate the affairs of the still living practitioner. They can come again in the bodies of the new born. The Great Mothers and the Grand Fathers swim in the salty waters of the birth canal, seeking once again the light of the Sun and Moon. In their coming, the covenant which contains all covenants is fulfilled. New issues from old in an unbroken spiral of universal flux. The last words of the dying echo in the infants' first cry. The play of the Divine Twins finds holy completion.

Get right with your ancestors! No statement deserves to be emphasized more than this. The ancestors are those who stand at your back. Their power flows through all that you perceive as you. Following are a few suggestions as to what is needed to join hands with the ancestors. Some general principals can be extracted from experience. Where the ancestors are involved there seems to be three conditions in point. There are the living ancestors, dead ancestors, and the practitioner as ancestor to those who come after.

Living ancestors should be treated with the honor that is the due of Elders. The living ancestor is an Elder who stands in a particularly special relationship to you.

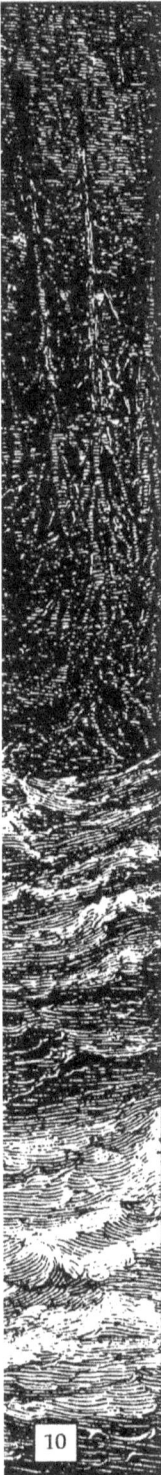

Remember them while they still live. They carry within them the stories and tales of your growing. They are the flesh in which you were formed.

A living ancestor may move in a way which you perceive as contradictory to your well being. If this happens, remove yourself from the sphere of those actions while continuing the larger relationship in its fullness. This is an act that requires much love and understanding on your part. There is no set formula which can be followed.

Dead ancestors are said to have passed into the waters beneath the earth. The waters enjoy both a symbolic and a literal existence. On a symbolic level the earth can conote physical existence and the waters can be compared to the racial consciousness. It is as if all that the ancestors have done and been is stored in the waters or racial consciousness and is thus available to the living. Literally, the waters exist in the same way that the personality of the ancestor exists. The waters are a coherent body of information possessed of, and influenced by, various currents of information. These currents are the ancestors. Integral to this information is a predisposition toward physical use and subtle, internal gratification.

> *And two long glasses brimmed with muscatel*
> *Bubble upon the table. A ghost may come;*
> *For it is a ghost's right,*
> *His(/her) element is so fine*
> *Being sharpened by his(/her) death,*
> *To drink from the wine-breath*
> *While our gross palates drink from the whole*
>   *wine.*
>   — From "All Souls Night" by W.B. Yeats; (/ her — Ed.)

Physical offerings provide pleasure to the ancestors and, at the same time, affirm that the ancestors are of use to the still living. The combination of food and drink is a powerful offering.

There is a beauty in preparing food for a loved one. If that food is part of a ritual remembering and feeding of an ancestor then the love flows in a particularly pure stream. The use of physical foods in a ritual meal has a strength beyond the vitalizing effects of the foods upon the ancestors. It is an expression of a warmth and an affirmation of a nearness which I have found, for myself, to be of transcendent beauty. The sharing of food is an ancient practice. It is a sacrament which strongly links all parts of the string of existence.

Once the food is offered it may be left on the altar or, after a time, eaten by the ritualist. One quickly develops a sense of what is appropriate to the individual situation. When the food is offered and then later eaten by the ritualist, aspects of the ancestor flow into the practitioner. A direct magickal link is created and power moves freely between the ancestor and the ritualist. It is as if the ancestors, in their eating, add a bit of themselves to the food. Food which is left on the altar is an act of pure giving. The ancestor(s) takes in all of the foods vitality and is nourished accordingly.

The practitioner is in the position of being an ancestor to those who will come after. The future arises irrevocably from the doings and empty spaces we create in the present. All time is now. Future lifetimes and future descendants throw their shadows back through time in a complicated web and in so doing, participate in their own becoming. The rites of the ancestors can reach into the future as well as the past. Future ancestors can find focus in present forms. The crossroad cuts into the future as well as into the past.

There are the ancestors and there are the dead taken as a whole. Which of the dead are not ancestors? Who is to be included in the ranks of the ancestors and why are they to be included? These questions speak directly to the "largeness" of the practitioner and can only be answered with an honesty that springs from the "self" in an unquestionable manner. In the greatest sense, all who

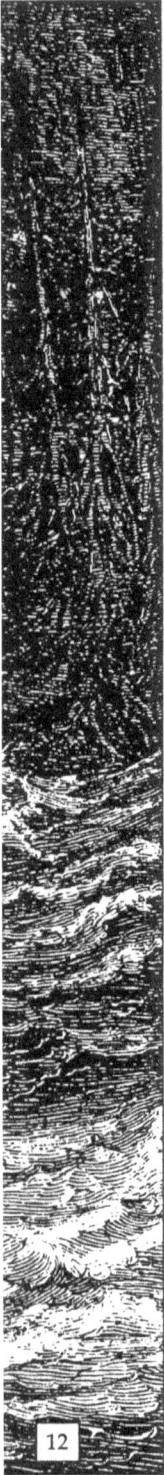

stand before us can be numbered as ancestors. All of the past, present, and future Mort stand in direct communication with us. All of the past, present, and future dead reach out to us.

This particular way of holding the dead brings into question the very concept of self. The concepts inherent in this formulation of "le Mort" stretch the horizons of our existence back through all past times and forward to include all future incarnations. The stuff of which we are composed encompasses a birth and death right that stretches beyond the continuum of infinity into eternity. Infinity being defined as encompassing all time and eternity being seen as a condition outside of time.[1]

Our existent selves are as a point in a web which reaches to the very limits of creation, there to be encompassed by the Marassa. We are the stuff of past, present, and future stars. The third or hidden twin is none other than ourselves. We are the space between the two twins as they reach to hold one another in eternal knowing.

---

[1]Distinction between infinity and eternity taken from a letter from Shambalah Nath to Purusas 252.

THE MYSTERIES

The Mysteries are the loa or deities. Deity is an apt word though it does not really capture the existential flavor of the loa. The word deity carries with it the connotation of distance; an entity which is far away and, in some manner, removed from the world. The loa, in the main, are never far removed from everyday life. Their voices speak through the effects of every action. Their presence is as integral to the practitioner's life as the very air which we breath. They have a quality which has been described by the feminist author and occultist Starhawk as immanence. Starhawk holds the Goddess as being immanent. This means that "she is within the entire living world." As such may the loa also be described. They are in all ways with us and, through the mechanism which has been misnamed as "possession", they communicate directly with their children.

Afrika stands as the planetary root home of the loa as well as of all members of our species. New loa are constantly being birthed in a world wide network. Voudoo, if it is anything, is oriented toward change. The loa arise from a number of sources; some of which are experiential. They may build an existence from the matrix of common physical needs and our responses to these needs. An example of this type of loa is Cousin Zaka who acts as a patron of peasant farmers. We need to cultivate crops in order to eat and Zaka directs this activity.

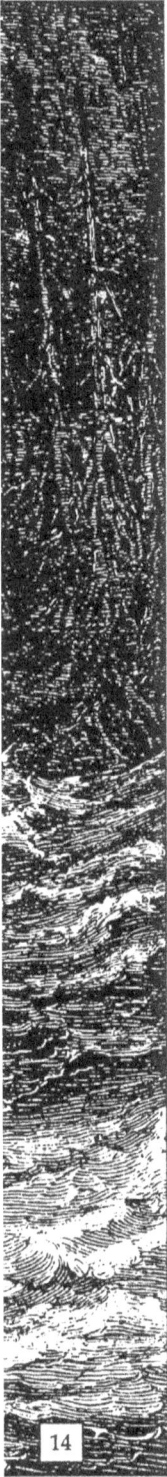

Along with physical, there are psychological needs. The sphere of love is looked after by Erzulie. In our being we search the aethers for subtle philosophical meaning. The loa Nanan Bouloucou is the grand mother of all the other loa and as such is the keeper of great philosophical mysteries as well as a loa of herbs and medicines. A loa may build itself from once living personages who, through the refinement of time and remembering, go through a process of clarification and come to embody some perfected attribute. The loa Shango, a once great Afrikan king, manifests through political and governmental functions.

"Possession" is possibly the most immediately dramatic form through which the loa manifest. It is the most fearful aspect of Voudoo to the New World mind. As such, the phenomenon deserves to be placed in a more tentable context.

"Possession" is most fearful if we view ourselves as static, fixed entities with an inborn mandate to resist all but superficial change. According to this view, "self" is a noun. The self is placed within the same category as a car or a house. It is a thing to possess or own. It is fearful to consider the possibility of a force taking our house away; in the same manner it is fearful to consider the loss of self. Self is seen as a little changing thing which we as beings possess.

An alternative perspective is afforded if self is placed within the linguistic context of "verb." The self held as verb has an ephemeral quality and is always changing. The mask[1] of the self is, at best, momentary. I have photos of myself as a child. I am no longer that self. I have memories of myself before I sat down to type. I am no longer that self. The being can wear any number of "masks" or "selves." It has been said that the one constant of existence is change. The phenomenon of "possession" is not a special case. It is an extreme point on the continuum of constant change.

14

[1]Nema; conversation, circa 1973.

According to the situation, some selves are more appropriate or convenient than others. "Possession" is in part characterized by a sudden change in the visible attributes of self; i.e. mannerism, memories, appearance, language, etc. Such a change might prove to be inconvenient while one is cashing a check in a bank. Such a change may be entirely appropriate in a ritual space which is constructed in a manner conducive to the change.

The largest religion in the western hemisphere is Christianity. Within the christian worldview, possession is almost always indulged in by demonic forces. God may send you to Hell, but he (sic) is not apt to possess you. Major exceptions to this are found in the "spiritist" christian denominations where speaking in tongues and being taken by the spirit is common. If you were raised as a christian (and not lucky enough to be of a spiritist denomination) the acceptance of "possession" as a valid expression of the religious impulse will require some deep unlearning of very early indoctrination. Perhaps "taken by the spirit" is a better general descriptor than "possession."

RITES

The qualities of Aeonic Voudoo are reflected in these rites. The loa, powers, etc., called are not pristine in the "traditional" sense. The practitioner is invited to touch and be touched by that which returns through the waters. We experience much more than we can ever explain or understand. Perform the rites as you will. Explain the results by your own wit. There is "that" which stands beyond and beckons.

The rites[1] of Voudoo can be divided into two major groupings or nations. There are the Rada rites and there are the Petro rites. The Rada rites call loa which are benevolent and lead the practitioner on an orderly path of development. These rites work the quarters of the crossroads. The Petro rites call loa whose benevolence can not be taken for granted and who lead the practitioner on a bit more circuitous path. Petro is possessed of tremendous power in that it melds two religious currents of extreme antiquity. In Petro is found a mixture of West Afrikan and Native Meso-American practices. The Rada rites are more those of the middle path while the Petro rites are more in the domain of magick and sorcery. Marassa Baphomet is Rada while the Spider Rite speaks more to the Petro branch.

[1]These rites are meant to serve as examples. All elements can be changed, individualized, etc.

MARASSA BAPHOMET (RADA)
An Individual Working

Marassa Baphomet by Purusas 252

The flow of this working is one of continuously more precise focus. In their turn, The Marassa, Legba, the Ancestors/Mort, and a Mysterie of the Marassa family (Marassa Baphomet) are called. It would be well to read the chapbook from cover to cover before performing this working.

Baphomet is the union of the male and female currents as they are perceived in the context of western magickal tradition. The diety can be attributed to Tarot trump number 15 (yod plus he). Baphomet is the androgyne.

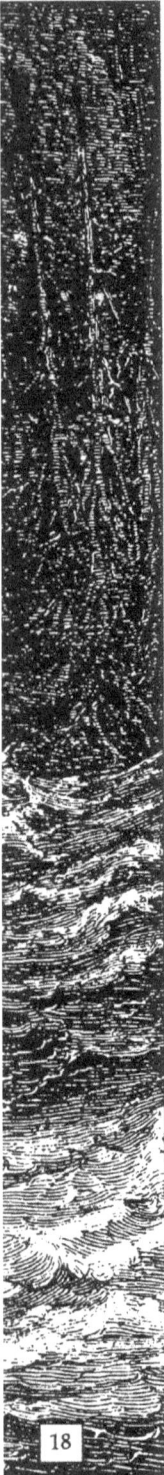

The glyph of Baphomet has been called "The Mystery of the Measure of Heaven and Earth." Symmetry is an essential quality of the Marassa. The word "symmetry" is synonymous with metron, meaning a measure. The marriage or joining of the Marassa and Baphomet is propitious in the extreme.

Tools: To the South - cornmeal and a drum.   To the North - a plate of food and a large cup of water. It is well if the cup contains both sweet and bitter waters. Add sugar for sweet and salt for bitter to prepare the water.

The Marassa

Enter the ritual space. Sit in the South and concentrate on the Marassa.

Take up the drum and play a rhythm which speaks to you of the Marassa. Use the drumming to bring concentration to the level of active trance. Concentration may be defined as an intense intellectual focus. Active trance is concentration with the addition of a strong emotional current.

Once active trance is reached, set the drum aside and image your hands as very young. Make the sign of the Marassa with both of your hands. The sign consists of spreading the small finger and the thumb as far apart as possible while bending the three mid fingers toward the palm of the hand. The thumb and small finger represent the Marassa. Next, bring the thumb and the small finger together while slowly unfolding the three mid fingers. The union of the Marassa is seen in the touching of the

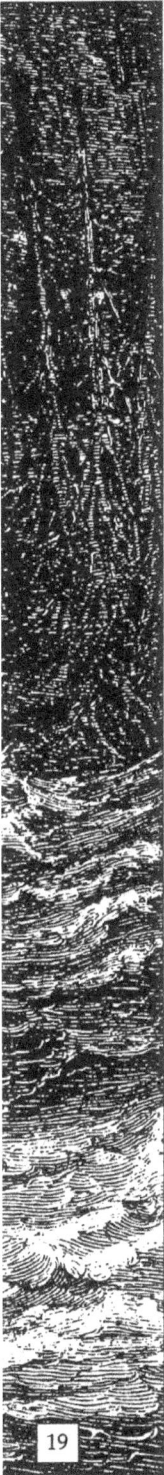

thumb and small finger. This is the completion of the gesture. The three mid fingers affirm the creation and existence of a third element which is the relation of the twins one to another.

Food & Water

Draw with
Left Hand

N

Draw with
Right Hand

S

Drum & Cornmeal

Finished Vèvè

Rise and move to the center of the ritual space. Construct the vèvè of the Marassa with the corn meal. Use the thumb and small finger of each hand to simultaneously draw the mirror elements of the vèvè.

Dance backwards[1] in a counterclockwise direction as a child in a dance of creation two times around the vèvè.

Seat yourself in the South.

Legba

Concentrate on Legba. Take up the drum and play a Legba rhythm. Move into active trance.

Set the drum aside and image your hands as very old.

Using your dominant hand, take a pinch of corn meal and bring it to your mouth. Breathe through your mouth

[1]Backwards dance/movement creates a powerful pull to draw the entities, as if through a mirror.

onto the cornmeal.[1]

Rise and draw the vèvè of Legba (crossroads) over the vèvè of the Marassa.

Dance backwards in a counterclockwise direction as an elder four times around the finished creation.

Ancestor / LeMort

The purpose of this section of the rite is to feed the ancestors and to call on their support in ritual workings.[2]

Move to the North. Raise the plate while holding it with both hands. Make the figure of the cross roads in the air.

After the figure is complete, kiss the plate and pass it through the center of the crossroads (drawn in the air) while saying words to this effect:

> *To all those whose Names are remembered.*
> *To all those whose Names are forgotten.*
> *I give you to eat.*
> *To all those who have come before.*
> *To all those who will come after.*
> *I offer sustenance.*

[1]Legba is the messenger of the loa; the carrier of the word. Air or breath is the medium of the word.

[2]An example of a daily Ancestor rite can be found in The Archives (see bibliography).

Hold the plate through the center of the crossroads and allow at least one bit of remembering to come into your thoughts. This could consist of a name, an incident, and/or a tale. If the name, etc. is not consciously recognizable it may originate from the future or long ago past. (Pay particular attention to names, etc. which repeat a number of times. This may indicate a special type of communication.)

Set the plate down and repeat the preceeding actions and words using the cup. Substitute "drink" for "eat."

Set the cup down and tell the ancestors/morts about the rite you are performing. Make the telling into a tale. Good, animated stories are always more appreciated than a dry recitation of events. Ask their assistance and return to the working you are performing.

Marassa Baphomet

At this point the vèvè should look like figure 1. In your mind, take all that you perceive of as the Marassa and combine the perception with that which is to you Baphomet. The relationship that is Marassa Baphomet is created in the cauldron of your being. Firmly establish this relationship in the alchemical retort of your mind, emotions, and body. Physically rise from the point of the relationship and combine the vèvè of Baphomet with the existing design. The result will look like figure 2.

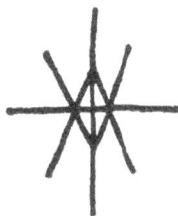

fig. 1   fig. 2

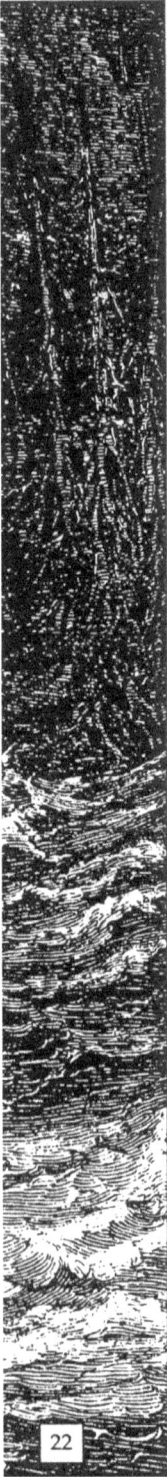

Stand to the east side of the vèvè. Allow its power to flow into you.

Upon first feeling this power, step backwards INTO the vèvè and dance as a young goat. As the vèvè is scattered, it will reformulate itself in your soul. Let the power exhaust itself through you.[1]

Exit the vèvè to the West.

Give thanks and leave the working space when the power has exhausted itself.

[1] If for some reason, you wish to dispel the power, the mere thought of separation from the entity will drive it from your being. Marassa Baphomet is tenuous in manifestation. The Mysterie "flees" at any sign of antagonistic separation in that its nature is that of perfect symmetry.

SPIDER RITE (PETRO)

Based on a series of rites initiated and
performed by Purusas 252 with Bate Cabal

Drawn by Akoko
Attributions based on "777" (see bibliography).

The purpose of this rite is to gain familiars or personal working spirits. These spirits take the form of spiders which inhabit the four cross quarters. The spiders' position as loa has, at times, been disputed. They may express themselves more through the category of astral mechanism.

The strategy of the rite consists of offering oneself as food for the spiders. The spiders come and eat. In so doing they absorb sufficient "fluids" so as to form a strong magickal link. Once the link is established, the will of the magician flows into the spiders. They grow heavy and fall into the domain of the magician. After they have been absorbed by the magician, they can be used as vehicles for etheric travel. In the form of the spiders, the magician can travel a web transversing etheric spaces and attain to experiences available in no other manner.

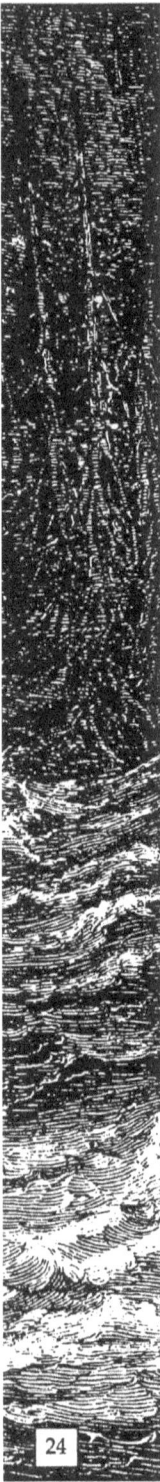

A word of caution. The rite can only be safely performed by an individual who has a firm grounding in will.[1] Will can be seen as a commitment to doings which are appropriate to one's unique situation in the body of the universe. In a very real sense, the magician is the center of her/his own web.

The Spider Rite is a group ritual and is optimaly performed by five ritualists though it may be performed with as few as two.

Tools: To the north and south place those items listed under Marassa Baphomet. In each of the four cross quarters place a cup of water. Toward the center of the work space place four instruments/objects which can be used to create a rhythm, incense of an offensively sweet odor, a black powder with which to draw a vèvè on the chest of the magician, and chains. Light the incense before the rite. Allow enough time for the smoke to fill the space.

The ritualists enter the working space as a group. The assistants seat themselves off to the side.

The magician calls the Marassa, Legba, and the Mort/Ancestors as described in the rite of Marassa Baphomet.

The magician lies down in the center of the Marassa/Legba vèvè s/he has constructed and is bound with chains by the assistants.

One of the assistants draws this vèvè on the chest of the

[1] *"The distance between what you think your will is and what it really consists of is bridged by what you are actually doing."* -Be'er Kayam Ben Barak; conversation in Cincinnati, 1986.

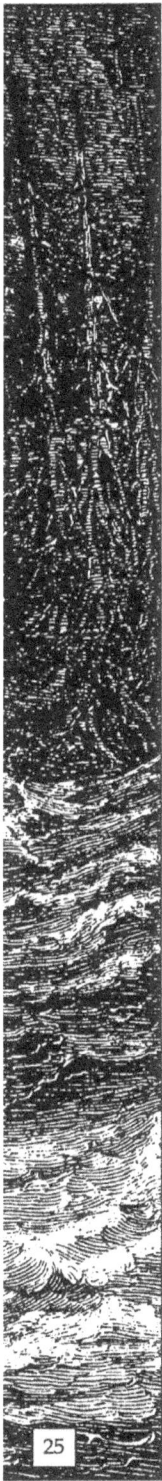

magician while the other assistants drum in a Petro rhythm. That is, a rhythm which emphasizes the off beats.

Once the vèvè is completed the assistants assigned to the cross quarters move to their positions taking with them their instruments.

The assistants call forth the spiders. This may be done by lifting the cup of water and visualizing the form of the spider of the particular cross quarter on the surface of the water. The water takes on the virtue of venom. The venom is then sprinkled in a line toward and touching the magician.

The visualization and order of the calling is as follows:

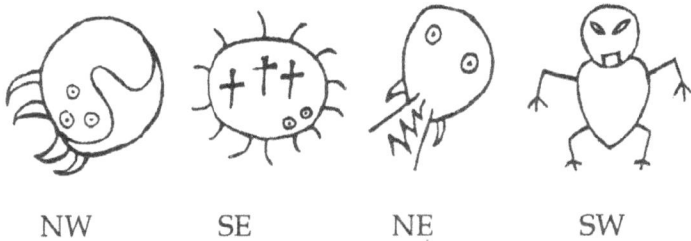

| NW | SE | NE | SW |

Once these acts are performed, the assistants may drum for a time in the Petro style. They then darken any lights, candles, etc. and leave the working space.

After about twenty minutes, they return and unfasten the magician. They then depart the space again.

The magician rises and leaves the temple when the power called by the rite has been taken in and, to some extent, balanced.

An assistant re-enters the working space. S/he gathers the cornmeal used in the Marassa/Legba vèvè and presents it to the magician.

BIBLIOGRAPHY

THE ARCHIVES; Black Moon Publishing, Box 19469, Cincinnati, Ohio, 45219-0469, USA. (In particular, Archives List #3)

CULTS OF THE SHADOW; Kenneth Grant; Samuel Weiser, Inc., 1976, USA.

DANCES OF HAITI; Katherine Dunham; Center for Afro-American Studies, 1983, USA.

DIVINE HORSEMEN, The Living Gods of Haiti; Maya Deren; McPherson and Company, 1953, USA.

HAITI SINGING; Harold Courlander; Cooper Square Publishers, 1973, USA.

JAMBALAYA, The Natural Woman's Book of Personal Charms and Practical Rituals; Luisah Teish; Harper & Row, 1985, USA.

MICHAEL BERTIAUX; La Couleuvere Noire, Chicago, USA.

SOCIÈTÈ; A Journal dedicated to the preservation and practice of Voudoun and other Neo-African religious systems. Technicians of the Sacred, Suite 310, 1317 N. San Fernando Blvd., Burbank, CA 91504.

TALES OF YORUBA GODS AND HEROES; Harold Courlander; Crown Publishers, Inc., 1973, USA.

777; Aleister Crowley; Samuel Weiser, Inc., 1977, USA.

NEW ORLEANS VOODOO TAROT; Louis Martinié and Sallie Ann Glassman, Destiny Books, 1992, USA. Book and 78 cards available from Black Moon Publishing, book signed and sigilized by the author, $29.95 plus $3.00 for 2 day Priority Post.

RECORDINGS/FILMS

CHEREL ITO; 106 Bedford St., #4, New York, New York, 10014, USA. Distribution for the film, DIVINE HORSEMEN; the records and books of Maya Deren.

FOLKWAYS RECORDS; 701 Seventh Avenue, New York, New York, 10036, USA.

LYRICHORD RECORDS; 141 Perry St., New York, New York, 10014, USA.

MYSTIC FIRE VIDEO; 24 Horatio St., #3, New York, New York, 10014, USA. Phone: 212-645-2733. (DIVINE HORSEMEN in video format.)

෨ඦ

All the individuals referred to in conversation may be reached c/o BLACK MOON PUBLISHING. They and the author invite comment.

෨ඦ

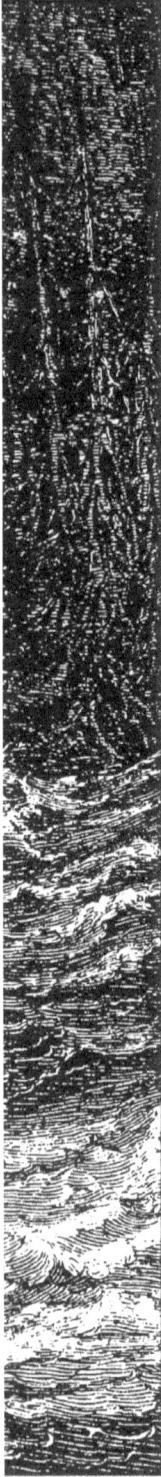

www.ingramcontent.com/pod-product-compliance
Lightning Source LLC
Chambersburg PA
CBHW030816090426
42737CB00010B/1298